# A New True Book

# THE CHOCTAW

### By Emilie U. Lepthien

Consultant: Robert B. Ferguson
Tribal Historian
Mississippi Band of Choctaw Indians

CHILDRENS PRESS ®
CHICAGO

## PHOTO CREDITS

© Julie Kelsey—2, 29 (2 photos), 32 (right), 45 (bottom right)

© Emilie Lepthien—2, 7 (2 photos), 17, 19 (right), 24, 28 (2 photos), 30, 31 (2 photos), 32 (left), 33 (2 photos), 34 (2 photos), 35 (2 photos), 45 (upper right)

Mississippi State Historical Museum—19 (left)

Mississippi Department of Archives and History—12

The Newberry Library, Chicago—21

New Orleans Museum of Art—4

The Oklahoma Historical Society—11

Photri—14

© John Running Photographs—8, 9, 23, (2 photos), 26, 36 (2 photos), 37 (2 photos), 38 (2 photos), 41, 42 (2 photos), 43 (3 photos), 45 (left)

*To the Choctaw Indians, who have faced every adversity but retained their culture, pride, and honor.*

Library of Congress Cataloging-in-Publication Data

Lepthien, Emilie U. (Emilie Uttig)
  The Choctaw.

  (A New true book)
  Includes index.
  Summary: A brief history of the Choctaw Indian tribe.
  1. Choctaw Indians—Juvenile literature.
[1. Choctaw Indians.  2. Indians of North America]
I. Title.
E99.C8L47  1987     973'.0497     87-14583
ISBN 0-516-01240-1

Childrens Press®, Chicago
Copyright ©1987 by Regensteiner Publishing Enterprises, Inc.
All rights reserved. Published simultaneously in Canada.
Printed in the United States of America.
1 2 3 4 5 6 7 8 9 10 R 96 95 94 93 92 91 90 89 88 87

JUL  '88

# TABLE OF CONTENTS

The Peaceful Choctaw...5

Peaceful Times...8

Intruders on Their Land...13

An Independent Nation...16

Education and Religion...18

More Treaties...20

Indian Territory...23

Problems Arise...25

The Eastern or Mississippi Band of
   Choctaw Indians...27

Choctaw Nation of Oklahoma...39

Culture...41

Government...44

Words You Should Know...46

Index...47

This painting, done by Alfred Boisseau in 1847, shows ancestors of the Choctaw walking along a bayou (marshy inlet of a river or lake).

# THE PEACEFUL CHOCTAW

*Chahta Hapia Hoke*, "We are the Choctaw," a proud Indian tribe declares.

For generations the Choctaw lived in Alabama and Mississippi. Like other Indian tribes they had no written records. Their legends told their tribal history. One legend told about how the Choctaw chose a place to settle.

The tribe came from the northwest. The prophets

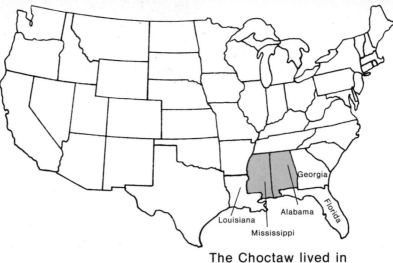

The Choctaw lived in
Alabama and Mississippi.

had said there was fertile
land and good hunting in
the east. Their leader,
Chahta, carried a sacred
pole. The sacred pole
would tell them where to
settle.

Each night Chahta drove
the pole into the ground.
Each morning the pole

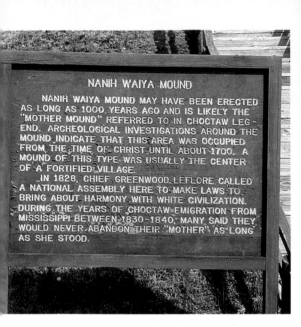

### NANIH WAIYA MOUND

NANIH WAIYA MOUND MAY HAVE BEEN ERECTED AS LONG AS 1000 YEARS AGO AND IS LIKELY THE "MOTHER MOUND" REFERRED TO IN CHOCTAW LEGEND. ARCHEOLOGICAL INVESTIGATIONS AROUND THE MOUND INDICATE THAT THIS AREA WAS OCCUPIED FROM THE TIME OF CHRIST UNTIL ABOUT 1700. A MOUND OF THIS TYPE WAS USUALLY THE CENTER OF A FORTIFIED VILLAGE.

IN 1828, CHIEF GREENWOOD LEFLORE CALLED A NATIONAL ASSEMBLY HERE TO MAKE LAWS TO BRING ABOUT HARMONY WITH WHITE CIVILIZATION. DURING THE YEARS OF CHOCTAW EMIGRATION FROM MISSISSIPPI BETWEEN 1830-1840, MANY SAID THEY WOULD NEVER ABANDON THEIR "MOTHER" AS LONG AS SHE STOOD.

Nanih Waiya Mound, as it is today

leaned to the east. Finally, at Nanih Waiya the pole stood upright. Chatha said this was the place to stay. There they built their homes and a sacred burial mound. Some Choctaw live near Nanih Waiya, Mississippi, today.

# PEACEFUL TIMES

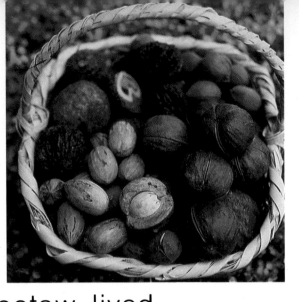

Hickory nuts and walnuts

The Choctaw lived peacefully as farmers for hundreds of years. They raised corn, beans, squash, melons, and pumpkins. Farm tools were made from stone, wood, or bone.

They gathered fruits, nuts, and berries. They hunted wild game with bows and arrows. The

A blowgun, made from swamp cane, was used to hunt small game.

boys used blow guns to bring down birds. Fish were caught with nets, spears, and arrows.

The Choctaw never wasted food. They shared extra corn, fish, and game with neighbors. The forest was precious. They made only narrow paths through the trees.

To build their cabins they drove poles close together into the ground. The poles were tied together with strong vines. Strips of cane filled the spaces between poles. Then mud was used to cover the cane. Roofs were thatched or covered with cypress or pine bark. Holes in the roof let the smoke out.

Clay bowl from the 1830s

   Cooking was done mostly outdoors in earthen pots over an open fire. Dishes and spoons were made of wood, shells, or bison horns.

   Beds lined the walls. They were raised and covered with cane. The beds also served as tables and chairs.

A Choctaw sharecropper family in 1937

These hardworking farmers were peaceful. But they fought fiercely when they were attacked.

# INTRUDERS
# ON THEIR LAND

In 1540 strange men entered Choctaw land. Some of the men rode animals. The Choctaw had never seen horses. They had never seen armor.

The strange men were from Spain. Their leader was Hernando De Soto.

At Maubilia, the Spaniards fought the

Mobile Choctaw. The
Indians fought bravely. But
their arrows could not cut
through Spanish armor.
Hundreds of Choctaw
warriors were killed, but
the battle stopped the
Spaniards' attack.

For another 150 years

the Choctaw had few contacts with white men. But by 1700, there were white settlers nearby.

For a time, the Choctaw were under the control of French governors. Then in 1763, the land came under British rule.

European settlers later called the Choctaw one of the Five Civilized Tribes. The Five Civilized Tribes were the Choctaw, Creek, Cherokee, Seminole, and Chickasaw.

# AN INDEPENDENT NATION

In January 1786, the United States government recognized the independent Choctaw Nation.

Four acts of Congress regulated relations between the Choctaws and settlers. Hunting and

River near Nanih Waiya

settling on Indian lands
was forbidden. The
Choctaws thought they
had found a government
that would guarantee their
rights.

# EDUCATION
# AND RELIGION

The Choctaw asked for
a Christian mission by
1819. Missionaries Cyrus
Byington and Alfred Wright
worked with the Folsoms,
two Choctaw Indians.
Together they translated
part of the Bible and
hymns into Choctaw.
Reverend Byington also
put together a Choctaw

First Choctaw dictionary, 1852 (left). Today, Choctaw children learn from books printed in their native language (right) as well as in English.

grammar, speller, and dictionary.

The missionaries started schools. By 1830 there were 11 schools, 29 teachers, and 260 students. About 250 adults were being taught to read their native language.

# MORE TREATIES

The Choctaw Nation had adopted laws based on United States law.

From 1801 to 1830, six more treaties were signed. Each time, the Choctaw gave up more land to the United States. President Andrew Jackson wanted the land for American settlers. In the 1820 treaty, more land in the west was open to them.

Pushmataha, a Choctaw chief, took part in treaty negotiations between the Choctaw Nation and the United States.

In the 1830 Treaty of Dancing Rabbit Creek, the Choctaw Nation lost the last of its eastern land. They were told to move to Indian Territory (Oklahoma). In all, they traded 23 million acres in Mississippi for 13 million acres in Oklahoma.

About 20,000 Choctaw lost land by this treaty. Over 8,000 decided to stay in Mississippi and claim land.

On the 350-mile journey to Indian Territory, one-fourth of the 12,000 Choctaw died of hunger, disease, and bitter winter weather. When they reached their new land, they had no tools, cattle, or seed to begin farming.

# INDIAN TERRITORY

Finally, when they could farm, the hardworking Choctaw raised pecans, cotton, corn, and other vegetables. They traded some crops for other goods.

Hickory corn (below) and a primitive corn used in making popcorn (left) are displayed in baskets made from swamp cane.

Head Start classroom at Pearl River Reservation

They started schools. The Choctaw wanted to learn English. It was easy to translate their language into English. Fortunately, however, they continued to speak, read, and write in Choctaw in both Oklahoma and Mississippi.

# PROBLEMS ARISE

When the Civil War began, the Choctaw sided with the southern states. However, they did little fighting.

When the South was defeated, the Choctaw resumed relations with the United States. However, things had changed. Many of the families were very poor. While the men had been in the army, thieves had taken their cattle.

Choctaw clothing of 1911

Their villages in Oklahoma were attacked by Plains Indians.

By 1907, the Choctaw Nation in the west became a part of the state of Oklahoma. It was no longer independent.

# THE EASTERN OR MISSISSIPPI BAND OF CHOCTAW INDIANS

The Mississippi Band lived in poverty. By 1900 many were sharecroppers. The land they had once owned (nearly 500 square miles) had been taken away.

By 1930 only 1,162 Choctaw lived in Mississippi. Today there

The office of the tribal chief at Pearl River Reservation (left) is separate from other tribal offices (right).

are about 6,000. The Eastern Choctaw live in seven small reservation communities near Philadelphia, Mississippi. The land is held in trust by the U.S. government. A land of hills and ravines, it is not good for modern farming methods.

Choctaw Central High School Homecoming Queen (left)
and Tribal Chief Phillip Martin (right)

Phillip Martin was
elected chief of the
Mississippi Band. He saw
the need to preserve tribal
culture by making the
reservation self-sufficient.

A worker prepares wires to be installed in automobile electrical systems.

He contacted large
companies. He told them
that the Choctaw were
hardworkers. Today there
are factories where such
different items as electrical
wiring for cars and trucks,
radio speakers, and
greeting cards are

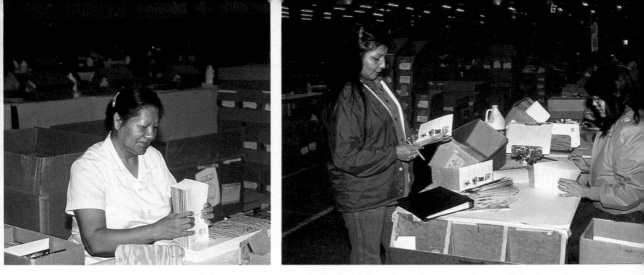

This greeting card factory is one of several small industries located in an Industrial Park area of the reservation.

assembled. Hundreds of Choctaw are employed.

The Mississippi Band has buses to bring the Choctaw from the communities to the factories at Pearl River, Redwater, and DeKalb.

The tribe also has buildings for job training,

New housing, built by tribal workers (left),
and a dental clinic (right)

food distribution, and bus maintenance. The tribe's development company has built six hundred new homes and renovated over 100 more. Classrooms, community buildings, and the Choctaw Health Center were built by this tribal

The Choctaw health center (left) and a nurse's aid (above)

company. There are plans to build a shopping center too.

A modern hospital and health care center is operated by the tribe. A new home for retired senior citizens is planned.

Each year during Arbor
Week, the tribe plants
oak and pine seedlings.

Pine trees are cut down
and made into paper pulp.
The tribe plants as many
as 40,000 Florida slash
pine seedlings in a year.
Twenty years from now
they will be ready to cut.
Day care, Head Start,
elementary schools, a high

The Bureau of Indian Affairs operates the public school on Pearl River Reservation (left). An elementary school on the Bogue Chitto Reservation (right)

school, and adult
education classes serve
the people. There are
several churches.

Each year since 1949,
the Mississippi Band holds
a Choctaw Indian Fair. In
this way they preserve
their heritage and culture.
The young men play

Among the many activities taking place at the annual Choctaw Indian Fair are stickball (left) and basket weaving (right).

stickball, the oldest ball game in America. Many people exhibit their bead-work and basketry. Tribal dances and songs are performed. The women wear their traditional multicolored dresses,

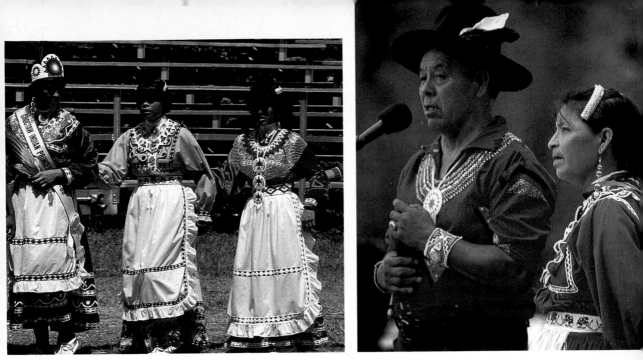

Colorfully dressed dancers (left) respond to the chants
of traditional singers (right).

ribbons, and beads. The
men wear colorful shirts,
black felt hats, and belts
trimmed with ribbons.

In World War I, Choctaw
soldiers spoke Choctaw
when they radioed
information to the soldiers

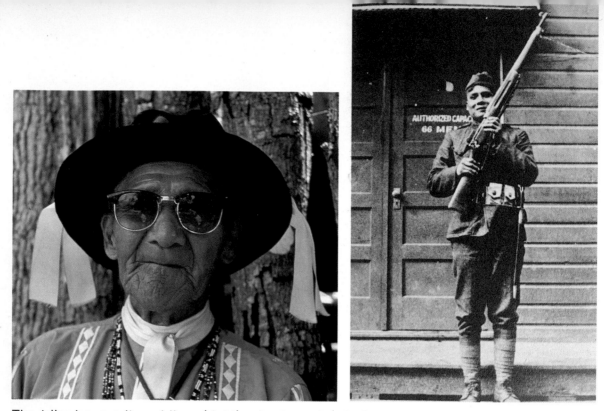

The tribe honors its soldiers (right), who have fought bravely in war, as well as its elders (above), who preserve the wisdom and history of the tribe.

in the front lines. The Germans heard these radio messages, but could not "break" the American code. The Choctaw soldiers helped America win battles.

# CHOCTAW NATION OF OKLAHOMA

Choctaw population in Oklahoma is about 20,000. Their first capitol was built in 1838 at Tushkahoma. Rebuilt twice, it is now a museum. The present headquarters is at Durant. The chief is Hollis E. Roberts. There are seven field officers in other counties.

The tribe owns and operates Arrowhead Resort Hotel on a lovely lake. Since 1978, there have been Head Start programs. The hospital in Talihina is run by the Choctaw Nation.

The Board of Agriculture operates a 2,627-acre ranch. Nutrition, food distribution, senior citizen services, social services, housing, and education are important Choctaw programs.

# CULTURE

Every Labor Day
weekend, the tribe holds a
festival at Tuskahoma.

Festival dances honor
the eagle, duck, quail,
raccoon, and snake. Both
men and women dance.

Teams from different areas compete in the annual stickball tournament. Each team has its own drummer (far right) to provide support.

A chanter leads the dancers. The only instruments are the drum and sticks for beating together.

Stickball games are played. The ball is made of deerskin. Hickory sticks, or *kapucha*, three feet

Stickball is played with
two small sticks (top left)
and a ball made from
strips of cow hide (above).

long, are used. A team
scores when it scoops up
the ball and throws or
touches it against its own
goalpost.

Stickball world
championships are held
each year in Mississippi.

# GOVERNMENT

Both the Mississippi and Oklahoma Choctaw elect a chief and members of a tribal council. In 1945 the Mississippi Band approved its constitution. The Choctaw Nation of Oklahoma ratified its constitution in 1983.

Both groups administer most of their own affairs. There are small groups of Choctaw in Louisiana, Tennessee, and Illinois.

Tribal workers (above) in the Choctaw's development company build a new nursing home.

Through their own efforts the future is much brighter for a people who lost so much, but who retain their pride and culture.

## SOME CHOCTAW WORDS

Choctaw is a Muskogan language related to Cree, Chickasaw, Seminole, and Miccosukee.

Oklahoma (okla homa)
  Red people

Tuscaloosa (tushka lusa)
  Black Warrior

Neshoba (Nushoba)
  Wolf

Bogalusa (Bok lusa)
  Black River

Bogue Chito (Bok Chitto)
  Big River

Talahina (tali hina—rock road) Railroad

## FAMOUS CHOCTAW CHIEFS

Tuscaloosa:
  Tricked Hernando De Soto

Mushulatubbee:
  Encouraged children to attend school in 1819

Pushmataha:
  Died in Washington, D.C., in 1824 while negotiating a treaty regarding Choctaw land.

# WORDS YOU SHOULD KNOW

**adopted**(uh • DOP • tid) — accepted, taken over, made as one's own
**chanter**(CHAN • ter) — a singer; one who sings a simple song that has many words or syllables sung on each note
**code**(KOAD) — system of letters or words or signals that has a secret meaning
**defeated**(dih • FEE • tid) — beaten
**generation**(jen • er • RAY • shun) — the average period of time between births of parents and children or children and grandchildren; usually considered to be about 30 years for each
**independent**(in • dih • PEN • dint) — free, able to manage by oneself
**journey**(JER • nee) — a trip, travel
**mound**(MOUND) — a small hill, natural or created of earth, sand, gravel; burial ground

**native**(NAY • tiv) — born or living naturally in a certain place

**poverty**(PAHV • er • tee) — state of being poor

**ravine**(rah • VEEN) — deep, narrow valley, usually cut into the earth by flowing water

**renovated**(REN • oh • vay • tid) — repaired, made as new again

**reservation**(rez • er • VAY • shun) — land reserved by the government for special use, as for an Indian tribe

**resumed**(rih • ZOOMED) — started again; taken up where one stopped

**self-sufficient**(SELF suh • FISH • int) — able to provide for its own support and upkeep

**sharecropper**(SHAIR • krop • er) — tenant farmer who shares his crop with the landlord in payment of rent of his land

**thatched**(THATCHED) — covered with straw, reeds, large leaves, used on roofs

**trust**(TRUHST) — a legal title to property held by one party for the benefit of another

**vine**(VYNE) — plants having firm but slender, easily twisted stems

# INDEX

Alabama, 5
arrows, 8, 9, 14
basketry, 36
beadwork, 36
beans, 8
beds, 11
berries, 8
blow guns, 9
Board of Agriculture, 40
bows, 8
British, 15
Byington, Cyrus, 18
cabins, 10

cane, 10, 11
Chahta, leader, 6-7
Cherokees, 15
Chickasaw, 15
Christianity, 18
Civil War, 25
clothing, 36, 37
Congress, acts of, 16-17
constitution, 44
cooking, 11
corn, 8, 23
Creeks, 15

culture, 35, 41-43
cypress, 10
dancing, 36, 41-42
Dancing Rabbit Creek,
   Treaty of, 21
DeKalb, 31
DeSoto, Hernando, 13
development company,
   32
dictionary, 19
disease, 22
drums, 42
Durant, 39

Eastern Choctaw, 27-28
education, 18-19, 24, 35, 40
English, 24
factories, 30, 31
farming, 8, 22, 23, 25, 28
festival, 41
fishing, 9
Five Civilized Tribes, 15
food distribution, 32, 40
French, 15
fruits, 8
games, 42-43
grammar, 19
headquarters, 39
Head Start, 34, 40
Health Center, Choctaw, 32-33
horses, 13
hospital, 33
hotel, 40
hunting, 8, 17
Illinois, 44
independence, 16, 26
Indian Territory, 21, 22, 23
Jackson, Andrew, 20
job training, 31
kapucha, 42

land, 20, 21, 22, 27, 28
language, 19, 24, 37
legends, 5-7
Martin, Phillip, 29
Maubilia, 13
melons, 8
missionaries, 18, 19
Mississippi, 5, 7, 22, 24, 27, 28, 43, 44
Mississippi Band, 27, 29, 31, 35, 44
mud, building, 10
Nanih Waiya, 7
Nation, The Choctaw, 16, 20-21, 39-40, 44
nets, 9
nuts, 8
Oklahoma, 21, 22, 24, 26, 39-40, 44
Pearl River, 31
pecans, 23
Philadelphia, Mississippi, 28
pine trees, 34
Plains Indians, 26
pole, sacred, 6-7
population, 39
reading, 19, 24

Redwater, 31
religion, 18-19
reservations, 28, 29
Roberts, Hollis E., 39
schools, 19, 24, 34-35
Seminoles, 15
senior citizens, 33, 40
sharecropping, 27
Spain, 13
spears, 9
spoons, 11
squash, 8
stickball, 36, 42-43
Talihina, 40
Tennessee, 44
tools, farm, 8
trading, 23
treaties, 20-22
trees, 34
tribal council, 44
Tribes, Five Civilized, 15
United States, 16, 20, 25, 28
wild game, 8
Wright, Alfred, 13
writing, 24

## About the author

*Emilie Utteg Lepthien earned a BS and MA degree and a certificate in school administration from Northwestern University. She has worked as an upper grade science and social studies teacher supervisor and a principal of an elementary and upper grade center for twenty years. Ms. Lepthien also has written and narrated science and social studies scripts for the Radio Council of the Chicago Board of Education.*

*Ms. Lepthien was awarded the American Educator's Medal by Freedoms Foundation. She is a member of the Delta Kappa Gamma Society International, Chicago Principals Association and life member of the NEA. She has been a co-author of primary social studies texts for Rand, McNally and Co. and an educational consultant for Encyclopaedia Britannica Films. Ms. Lepthien has written Enchantment of the World books on Australia, Ecuador, and the Philippines.*

The number of books that may be drawn at one time by the card holder is governed by the reasonable needs of the reader and the material on hand.

Books for junior readers are subject to special rules.